class & climate

International Bolshevik Tendency

class & climate

First published 2020 by Bolshevik Publications

BCM Box 4771
London WC1N 3XX
Britain

www.bolshevik.org
ibt@bolshevik.org
Facebook: Bolsheviks
Twitter: @ibt1917

Cover image: *The Bones of Bamsebu, Svalbard, June 2009, Camille Seaman*

CONTENTS

CAPITALISM & CLIMATE CHANGE

Marxism vs. eco-reformism

OVER SIXTY YEARS AGO, in November 1959, the American Petroleum Institute co-sponsored a symposium at Columbia University in New York City to commemorate the U.S. oil industry's centennial year. Among the guest speakers was renowned physicist Edward Teller, who wa-rned the audience of scientists, government officials and industry representatives that burning large quantities of fossils fuels risked "contaminating the atmosphere" with carbon dioxide to such an extent as to provoke rising global temperatures:

> "Carbon dioxide has a strange property. It transmits visible light but it absorbs the infrared radiation which is emitted from the earth. Its presence in the atmosphere causes a greenhouse effect.... It has been calculated that a temperature rise corresponding to a 10 per cent increase in carbon dioxide will be sufficient to melt the icecap and submerge New York. All the coastal cities would be covered, and since a considerable percentage of the human race lives in coastal regions, I think that this chemical contamination is more serious than most people tend to believe."
>
> —*Guardian*, 1 January 2018

Teller's warning was based on a small but growing body of scientific research over the preceding decade that detailed the contribution of industrial activity to increases in atmospheric carbon dioxide (CO_2). By 1965, the U.S. President's Science Advisory Committee submitted a 20-page paper to Lyndon Johnson indicating that the growth in CO_2 emissions "may be sufficient to produce measurable and perhaps marked changes in climate" (Inside Climate News, 13 April 2016). Over the next two decades, as more and better data was analyzed by scientists around the world, a clear and unmistakable picture emerged of the consequences of increased emissions of various "greenhouse gases" (including CO_2, methane, nitrous oxide, chlorofluorocarbons and hydrofluorocarbons). It would result in not simply smog, acid rain and/or a thinning ozone layer but an average rise in global temperatures and qualitative changes to the climates and surface features that have sustained human life on Earth.

Most greenhouse gas emissions outside of natural processes (of which CO_2 accounts for 4/5 of the total) come from the burning of fossil fuels for industry and electricity production, though agriculture and transportation are also significant sources. Despite the contribution of hydro-electric and nuclear power to the energy needs of many countries, most electricity is still generated through the combustion of coal, natural gas and oil. Governments and private industry have made investments in renewable energy sources such as wind and solar power, but fossil fuels overwhelmingly dominate, especially in so-called developing countries. Commercial and private transportation continues to rely on combustion engines that burn oil products.

Unheeded Warnings

Although the dangers of burning coal, natural gas and oil have been clear for generations, our dependence on these non-renewable natural resources has grown, and continues to grow, on a global scale. In the three decades following the establishment of the Intergovernmental Panel on Climate Change (IPCC) in 1988, more greenhouse gases were pumped into the atmosphere than in the preceding 250 years combined (Carbon Majors Report 2017). Greenhouse gas emissions have grown at an annual rate of 1.5 percent over the past decade. Humans have added more than 1.6 trillion tons of CO_2 to the atmosphere since the industrial revolution (Center for Climate and Energy Solutions). At the time of the first coal-burning steam engines, the quantity of atmospheric CO_2 was 280 parts per million (ppm); that figure now stands at 412 ppm (NASA)—a level last seen 3 million years ago, when the Earth was on average 2°C–3°C warmer than it was in the immediate "pre-industrial" era (1850–1900) (climate.gov). All the extra

Tar sands petroleum extraction facility in Alberta, Canada. This industry is a major contributor to global greenhouse gas emmissions.

CO_2 in the atmosphere has so far led to a 1.1°C rise in global average temperatures compared with pre-industrial levels (IPCC).

Predicting future temperature increases is difficult owing in part to uncertainty over future emissions, as well as the complex nature of "tipping points" that trigger further acceleration of heating, e.g., the melting of the polar ice caps (which reflect sunlight back into space) and permafrost (which contains large amounts of methane) (*Guardian*, 9 October 2018). Nevertheless, the IPCC estimates that global warming will reach 1.5°C (over pre-industrial levels) sometime between 2030 and 2052. As we approach the year 2100, the pace of temperature increase is likely to quicken. In November 2019, the United Nations Environment Program published an Emissions Gap Report, which acknowledged that—even if countries fully meet the emissions targets ("unconditional NDCs" or Nationally Determined Contributions) set in the 2015 Paris Agreement—there is "a 66 per cent chance that warming will be limited to 3.2°C by the end of the century." Annual *reductions* of emissions by 7.6 percent, starting now, would be required merely to keep the global temperature increase to within 1.5°C. Otherwise, by the end of the century, global temperatures are likely to have risen by 2°C to 4°C, with most estimates somewhere around 3°C.

The consequences of such temperature increases range from catastrophic to cataclysmic. Climate-change writer David Wallace-Wells observes:

> "[A]nyone who sees a world of 3 degrees warming—or even 2.5 degrees—as a positive or happy outcome has a pretty grotesque, or at least deluded, perspective on human suffering. At just two degrees, the U.N. estimates, damages from storms and sea-level rise could grow 100-fold. Cities in South Asia and the Middle East that are today home to many millions of people would be so hot during summer heat waves, scientists have projected, even going outside during the day could mean risking heatstroke or heat death. The number of climate refugees could pass 200 million, according to the U.N., and more than 150 million would die from the impacts of air pollution alone. North of two degrees, of course, the strain accumulates and intensifies, and while some amount of human adaptation to these forces is inevitable, the scale of adaptation required at even two degrees begins to seem close to impossible."
>
> —*New York Magazine*, 20 December 2019

Profit vs. Planet

Future historians may look back on this period and puzzle over the recklessness with which humanity clung to practices we knew were unconscionably dangerous. But our persistent and deepening reliance on fossil fuels, although irrational from the standpoint of the preservation of our species, is "rational" from the standpoint of what actually drives our current economic system forward: the pursuit of profit by private companies competing with one another to stay in business and thrive in the short to medium term. The political and ideological power of these companies—in particular huge energy and industrial corporations that exploit fossil fuels—has been leveraged to ensure that our response to the threat of climate change has been tepid at best.

Big Oil has dumped a fortune into a disinformation campaign to protect shareholders' investments. The fossil fuel industry has been able to muddy the waters to the extent that only "about half of Americans (49%) say human activity contributes a great deal to climate change, and another 30% say human actions have some role in climate change. Two-in-ten (20%) believe human activity plays not too much or no role at all in climate change" (Pew Research Center). In Britain, although the vast majority of the population believes that climate change is real, only 36 percent think it is "mainly" or "entirely" caused by human activity—over half "think human and natural causes are equally to blame" (British Social Attitudes). The relative success of the fossil fuel industry's propaganda can in part be attributed to the use of social media in spreading misinformation and the (healthy and justified) skepticism ordinary people have toward mainstream news outlets. So mistrusted is the "Fourth

Workers clean coastal lands from BP oil spill in Gulf Shores, Alabama, June 2010.

Estate" of liberal corporate news that, even when they are reporting the truth, sensible people with limited time to investigate are more inclined to believe crackpot YouTube commentators.

In the U.S., oil and gas companies have given hundreds of millions of dollars in "campaign contribution" bribes to politicians at all levels of government (OpenSecrets.org). Approximately 28 percent of all members of the U.S. Congress purport not to believe in climate change (Center for American Progress Action Fund). The endemic corruption of the American political system—evident also in the stranglehold that Wall Street and the military-industrial complex have on Washington—is well-known. Yet the problem runs deeper. Unlike Philip Morris and other tobacco companies that waged a losing battle denying the link between smoking and cancer, ExxonMobil, Chevron, ConocoPhillips, Occidental Petroleum and their international competitors (e.g., BP, Royal Dutch Shell, Total SA, Gazprom) sell products that are central to the functioning of modern industrial economies.

Abandoning fossil fuels would not only deal a death blow to a powerful industry valued at nearly $5 trillion globally (Science Alert), it would also require the near-suspension of market mechanisms and the expropriation of thousands of large companies which would collapse outside of a concerted, centralized redevelopment of the entire world economy. When Donald Trump or other right-wingers suggest that the concept of human-made climate change is a hoax promoted by crypto-communist "globalists," they are unwittingly identifying the real culprit: capitalism.

Capitalism, Value & Growth

Liberals and social democrats advocate government intervention to boost "green" technologies and promote "carbon neutral" industrial development. Libertarians, insofar as they concern themselves at all with how the "free market" affects the environment, reject such an approach in favor of unleashing the entrepreneurial "genius" of the likes of Elon Musk to save the world. What both camps have in common is an unwillingness to eliminate private property in the means of production, transportation and communication. They refuse to see that the capitalist mode of production, which relies on such private property, is the root of the problem.

In theory, one may conceive of a form of capitalism that employs alternative energy sources. Yet capitalism does not exist "in theory" but in the real world, where there is an entrenched, immensely wealthy and extremely powerful fossil fuel industry. Even assuming a successful mass public pressure campaign to abandon coal, natural gas and oil as sources of energy, a reform-minded capitalist government would be confronted with the need to completely retool the world's industrial plant and replace all existing consumer and capital-goods products that emit greenhouse gases (e.g., automobiles) with zero-emission alternatives within the next *decade* to avoid a 1.5°C temperature rise. Market mechanisms and atomized private property in the means of production and transportation are simply incompatible with this goal. And even if they were compatible, capitalism could not afford the transition, since the downward pressure exerted on the profit rate by the initial phase of the shift would thrust the economy into depression. To recognize the economic limits of a "green industrial revolution" under capitalism is to understand why capitalism has brought us to the precipice of ecological collapse in the first place.

Beyond its privileging of short-term profit-making over long-term sustainability (and other rational objectives), capitalism has an inherent tendency to grow in a manner that necessarily disregards the human and natural elements of civilization. Karl Marx, the greatest theorist of capitalism and the foundational figure of the movement to topple it, understood capitalism, at root, to be a *mode of production*. Production is the process by which humans convert material nature into useful things, and it is fundamental to how we live our lives and organize society. Our social relations are deeply implicated in production, so that there is at least a rough correspondence between the social relations of production and the other ways we relate to one another, such as in family structures or politics.

For most of our existence as a species, we had more or less egalitarian relations of production—the surplus of what we were able to produce being so tiny that there was no material incentive for any segment of society to convert the means of production into exclusive private property. This changed about 10,000 years ago with the emergence of a large surplus product associated with the agricultural revolution in what we today call the Middle East. Since then, we have passed through different forms of class-divided society with distinct class-antagonistic modes of production. The latest and most productive class-divided mode of production is capitalism, which first emerged in Western Europe a few hundred years ago. (See Part II of *Celebrating Red October* (bolshevik.org) for a discussion of Marx's historical materialism and its relationship to the concept of revolution.)

While the "primitive" communalistic societies of hunters and gatherers often took their toll on the local environment as humans sought to survive by exploiting nature, it is really the advent of agriculture and, more fundamentally, the implication of class divisions in production that allowed our species to begin to alter the Earth in profound ways. Friedrich Engels, co-founder with Marx of "scientific socialism," summed up this history a century and a half ago:

> "Let us not, however, flatter ourselves overmuch on account of our human victories over nature. For each such victory nature takes its revenge on us. Each victory, it is true, in the first place brings about the results we expected, but in the second and third places it has quite different, unforeseen effects which only too often cancel the first. The people who, in Mesopotamia, Greece, Asia Minor and elsewhere, destroyed the forests to obtain cultivable land, never dreamed that by removing along with the forests the collecting centres and reservoirs of moisture they were laying the basis for the present forlorn state of those countries. When the Italians of the Alps used up the pine forests on the southern slopes, so carefully cherished on the northern slopes, they had no inkling that by doing so they were cutting at the roots of the dairy industry in their region; they had still less inkling that they were thereby depriving their mountain springs of water for the greater part of the year, and making it possible for them to pour still more furious torrents on the plains during the rainy seasons. Those who spread the potato in Europe were not aware that with these farinaceous tubers they were at the same time spreading scrofula. Thus at every step we are reminded that we by no means rule over nature like a conqueror over a foreign people, like someone standing outside nature—but that we, with flesh, blood and brain,

Sewage, full of heavy metals, pollutes aquifers in Africa's largest landfill in Lagos, Nigeria.

belong to nature, and exist in its midst, and that all our mastery of it consists in the fact that we have the advantage over all other creatures of being able to learn its laws and apply them correctly."

—"The Part played by Labour in the Transition from Ape to Man," May–June 1876

Capitalism, by massively increasing the "forces of production" (i.e., humanity's ability to transform nature), took this relationship to a new level, bringing us to the current crisis.

But it is not the growth of the productive forces per se that has led to environmental destruction and pushed us toward the verge of cataclysmic climate change. Rather, it is the particular *social logic* of the capitalist mode of production that is responsible.

What does the "social logic" of capitalism refer to? Every mode of production, including a future communist mode, rests on a basic "metabolic" relationship between humanity and non-human nature, i.e., a dialectical exchange of energy and matter. Humans seek to develop the productive forces with the aim of securing themselves against dangers presented by the natural environment, e.g., predators, hostile weather, scarcity of food. In this sense, there is an inherent tendency toward increases in our efforts to "control" nature. But this tendency does not exist in isolation from the social relations of production, which in fact play a determinative role in how, why and the extent to which the forces of production are developed. All class-divided modes of production involve a privileged ruling class encouraging, at least to some extent, the growth of productive capacities in a manner that is congruent with its own enrichment and leisure. Capitalism's particular variant of this social dynamic has led to a comparatively intense and reckless manner of productive force growth that has caused severe "metabolic rifts," including the climate crisis (see "Communism & Ecology," *1917* No.36, bolshevik.org). There are two interconnected aspects of capitalist social relations that are specifically responsible for this state of affairs.

First, capitalists compete with one another. In order to stay in business and thrive, a capitalist must capture markets and drive down the price of their products. The fragmentation of the capitalist ruling class, offset only partially by the sort of ideology that cohered previous ruling classes into a self-conscious cultural unit, means that the tendency toward market anarchy stemming from competition will eventually trump whatever collectivist environmental program the capitalist state may seek to implement in the common interests of the bourgeoisie. Not only do markets win out over economic planning in the long run, but those markets encourage competitors to aggressively seek to drive each other out of business.

Second, capitalism exhibits a tendency to drive down the cost of commodities (and thus compete in the market) by increasing labor productivity through the introduction of labor-saving technology. Under previous class-divided modes of production, the producing class was itself considered property (e.g., the ancient slave system) or held some ownership of the means of producing their own livelihood (e.g., European feudalism). These pre-capitalist social relations of production encouraged but also limited the extent of productive force growth. While they were brutally oppressive, their impact on the natural environment was checked to some extent by the perception of the ruling class—a perception grounded in the mode of production—that there was some value in maintaining the producing class (or at least in not simply discarding it in favor of technological development).

Capitalism, by contrast, exploits the labor of a producing class that has no "organic" connection to the ruling class—a producing class that instead enters into a relationship with the capitalists in a highly mediated form, i.e., a wage agreement that leaves the capitalists free to hire and fire workers on the basis of economic need (or other whims). These workers, from the standpoint of the capitalist, are just another expense — indeed, the most troublesome expense, since workers get sick, go on strike, demand higher pay, etc. Capitalists therefore aim to displace living labor from the production process by creating new technologies that can exploit natural resources in ever more efficient ways.

However, the capitalist mode of production obscures the connection between human labor and profit meaning that capitalists do not recognize the source of their own wealth. Under capitalism, the surplus product (which takes the form of profit, interest and ground rent) is simply the market-mediated expression of the surplus labor product, just as the wealth of the ruling classes in all previous class-divided modes of production was based on the exploitation of the producing classes and the natural environment. Economic value under capitalism must, therefore, be measured in terms of the quantity of generalized human labor required to produce a commodity. This continued reliance on human labor, coupled with the incessant drive to displace it from the production process, results in a general tendency for the rate of profit to fall, generating profitability crises as the system moves in contradiction and tends toward ever greater irrationality. (See Murray E.G. Smith, *Invisible Leviathan: Marx's Law of Value in the Twilight of Capitalism*, Haymarket 2019.)

By defining and determining growth strictly in terms of expanding value, capitalism is blinded to the fact that "Nature is just as much the source of use values (and it is surely of such that material wealth consists!) as labor, which itself is only the manifestation of a force of nature, human labor power" (Marx, *Critique of the Gotha Programme*).

Outside the restrictions imposed by capitalism, "growth" could conceivably

Capitalist "growth": expensive high-rise buildings overlooking poverty and privation in a slum in Mumbai.

be defined in terms of expanding human happiness. Its measure could involve some combination of material well-being (and the productive capacities undergirding it), sustainable interactions with non-human nature and social-psychological factors—but the promotion of any positive human development under a regime of capitalist growth is, at best, a fortunate and limited coincidence.

Capitalism has continued to exploit fossil fuels despite the fact that climate change could destroy humanity. It cannot do otherwise because there is no force emerging from the "logic" of the system itself that can privilege social or ecological rationality over the expansion of value. At the same time, the falling tendency of the rate of profit—which emerges out of the historical development of this system of self-expanding value—has also led to an economic impasse: capitalism could not afford to transition to a "green" future even if it could imagine such a transition in the first place.

Communism, Growth & Soviet 'Modernization'

One of Marx's greatest theoretical insights was that capitalism prepares its historical succession in very specific ways. The foundations of the next stage in human socio-economic evolution—a communist mode of production based on collaboration and the collective application of society's resources to meet human needs—can be seen in embryonic fashion in the large corporations that have come to dominate the capitalist economy. Freed from private ownership and placed under democratic control, the large-scale planning that already occurs within giant companies (and often across whole industries) could be expanded and reoriented to gradually bring our species into the first, or lower, stage of communism (i.e., "socialism"), where class relations disappear. Between capitalism and socialism lies a period of transition governed by a new form of state—the working-class majority organized as a force of control and planning—that will "wither away" as society approaches communism.

Alongside collectivization of the means of production, the material condition for the transition to socialism is a higher development of the productive forces. Society must be able to produce at such a level as to ensure an equality of abundance, i.e., every human being, with minimal productive output, must be guaranteed not only the basic material needs (food, shelter and clothing) but also the leisure time and resources to pursue non-material yet creative activities (intellectual, emotional, "spiritual," etc.) generating a sense of fulfillment. It is, therefore, necessary for there to be more growth.

But what would that growth look like? Would it merely be an expansion of the current growth model, which has disregarded the natural environment and led us into the climate change conundrum? For Marxists, the growth of the productive forces when extracted from the deforming influence of the pursuit of profit will have to include enhancing our capacity not simply to transform nature but to do so in ways that are inherently more human. In other words, there must be a qualitative, and not merely a quantitative, aspect to the transformation of human productive capacities as we move toward socialism.

For instance, a technology that dramatically reduces the collective labor time that we must allocate to building housing (e.g., with cheap timber) would not qualify as contributing to "socialist growth" if it necessarily entailed clearcutting forests, creating desolate landscapes and the loss of biodiversity. Truly "mastering nature" (i.e., achieving a high level of transformative capacity) must include being able to make conscious choices about how to transform nature so that we actually want to live in the world we construct around us. Socialist goals will surely involve such principles as respecting human individuality and the natural environment, and they will be infused with an ethos of cooperation and responsibility across generations. Something along these lines is indicated in Marx's *Economic and Philosophic Manuscripts of 1844*, where he describes communism as:

> "the genuine resolution of the conflict between man and nature and between man and man—the true resolution of the strife between existence and essence, between objectification and self-confirmation, between freedom and necessity, between the individual and the species. Communism is the riddle of history solved, and it knows itself to be this solution."

Particularly in the generations before climate change had been established by science, Marxists sometimes presented the need for growth of the productive forces without sufficiently distinguishing it from its form under capitalism. Lenin once quipped that "Communism is Soviet power plus the electrification of the whole country, since industry cannot be developed without electrification." He was, of course, not speaking literally; his point was that industrialization—and the development of the energy sources it required, which at the time included coal—was central to the transition to socialism, which he and every other Marxist understood could only be achieved on a global scale. The Soviet Union never achieved socialism, nor could it do so on its own. A relatively underdeveloped country at the time of the October Revolution, Russia found itself isolated on the world stage, cut off from international economic integration with the failure of revolutions in other parts of the globe. Under these conditions, a political counterrevolution had occurred by the mid-1920s, in which the revolutionary wing of the Soviet government was defeated by a bureaucracy that continued to rest on an increasingly degenerated expression of collectivized property.

The history of the Soviet workers' state, particularly in its early phase under the leadership of Lenin, demonstrated a complicated attitude toward growth and the environment. Spurred on by the need to catch up to the advanced capitalist countries (i.e., "modernize") and surpass their level of development (all while promoting revolutionary overturns that would eventuate in linking up their economies in the short to medium term), the Bolsheviks' policy was aimed at a robust pace of industrialization tempered more by the need to achieve balanced economic growth, and changing the class composition of society, than by environmental concerns. The fierce and important struggle within the Communist Party during the 1920s between the revolutionary faction headed by Leon Trotsky and the bureaucratic faction headed by Joseph Stalin paid little attention to the question of the environment.

With the defeat of Trotsky's Left Opposition, which favored a steady pace of industrialization over the bureaucracy's encouragement of agrarian expansion, the country's economic problems led Stalin, in an abrupt turnabout, to implement forced collectivization and an overly-rapid industrialization program beginning in the late 1920s and early 1930s. The result was an impressive and unprecedented expansion of industrial capacity, as Trotsky reported in *The Revolution Betrayed*:

> "[The Soviet Union's] industrial production has increased during this same period [1929–1935] approximately 3½ times, or 250 per cent. The heavy industries have increased their production during the last decade (1925 to 1935) more than 10 times. In the first year of the first five-year plan (1928 to 1929), capital investments amounted to 5.4 billion rubles; for 1936, 32 billions are indicated.
>
> "...The output of oil, coal and iron has increased from 3 to 3½ times the pre-war figure. In 1920, when the first plan of electrification was drawn up, there were ten district power stations in the country with a total power production of 253,000 kilowatts. In 1935, there were already ninety-five of these stations with a total power of 4,345,000 kilowatts. In 1925, the Soviet Union stood eleventh in the production of electro-energy; in 1935, it was second only to Germany and the United States. In the production of coal, the Soviet Union has moved forward from tenth to fourth place."

This staggering growth—at a time when the capitalist economies had sunk into the Great Depression—came at a great human and ecological

Anatoly Lunacharsky, People's Commissar of Education (1917-1929), responsible for establishing the zapovedniki ecological reserves.

cost. In the decades that followed, little attention was paid to the environmental devastation wrought by Stalinist planners. Nor was there any effective push-back from the population in a bureaucratic system that had strangled workers' democracy. Before its demise in 1991, the Soviet Union was the second industrial power on Earth; it was also one of the worst polluters, as its leaders demonstrated a criminal disregard for the environment. The Aral Sea, once the fourth largest freshwater lake on the planet, was reduced to a quarter of its size due to the diversion of water for irrigation projects (today it is a mere one-tenth of its original size).

Yet central economic planning, both in the Soviet republic's revolutionary phase and in the era of Stalinist political counterrevolution, also revealed its capacity to address environmental issues. While fossil fuel induced climate change was not yet known, there were other environmental concerns, including deforestation. John Bellamy Foster observes:

"Immediately after the October 1917 Revolution, Lenin supported the creation of the People's Commissariat of Education under the leadership of Anatolii Vasil'evich Lunacharskii, which was given responsibility for conservation. In 1924 the All-Russian Conservation Society (VOOP) was created with an initial membership of around one thousand. The Education Commissariat with Lenin's backing set up the celebrated ecological reserves, known as zapovedniki, of relatively pristine nature, set apart for scientific research. By 1933 there were thirty-three zapovedniki encompassing altogether some 2.7 million hectares."

—*Monthly Review*, 1 June 2015

One of the most significant lasting contributions of the Soviet Union may be the work done by its scientists, some of whom pioneered the study of climate change from the 1950s, as Foster explains:

"Soviet climatologists discovered and alerted the world to the acceleration of global climate change; developed the major early climate change models; demonstrated the extent to which the melting of polar ice could create a positive feedback, speeding up global warming; pioneered paleoclimatic analysis; constructed a new approach to global ecology as a distinct field based on the analysis of the biosphere; originated the nuclear winter theory; and probably did the most early on in exploring the natural-social dialectic underlying changes in the earth system."

—*Monthly Review*, 1 June 2015

Marxists defended the Soviet Union despite and against the ruling Stalinist bureaucracy. We do not celebrate the contributions it made to climate change, but we understand the historical conditions that led to its industrial model, and we fought the degeneration of the revolution. It was the destruction of workers' democracy under the Stalinists that made possible the environmentally irresponsible manner in which the country was developed.

Similarly, we today understand why China—a deformed workers' state modeled on the Stalinist Soviet Union—pursues rapid industrialization. On the one hand, it is the product of imperialist-driven "globalization," as firms in rich capitalist states relocate production to low-wage areas in China and other countries. On the other, it results from domestic "modernization" plans, as the regime in Beijing seeks to leverage its access to advanced technology to develop industries to meet its needs. China is the world's leading contributor of greenhouse gas emissions: of the nearly 35 gigatons of CO_2 that were pumped into the atmosphere in 2017, approximately 10 gigatons came from China (almost twice as much as the U.S., the next single biggest national contributor) (China Power, 19 July 2018). Although China pales in comparison to the U.S. on a per capita basis, there is no question that the fundamentally non-capitalist economy of China is a major contributor to climate change.

Yet it is neither state ownership nor economic planning that is the cause of the abysmal environmental record of China (or, before it, the Soviet Union). To the contrary, these elements of the degenerated and deformed workers' states are what revolutionaries defend. Both collective ownership and planning are essential to averting climate catastrophe and improving the lives of human beings and should be quantitatively and qualitatively expanded. Our species' failure to do so on a global scale has created the conditions in which stunted transitions to socialism (i.e., deformed workers' states) are forced to crudely mimic the "modernizing" growth model of capitalism.

The imperialist system also demonstrates criminal disregard for the environment in those neocolonial countries where its corporations exploit workers and pollute the air, water and land with virtually no restraints. Fighting climate change requires a struggle that focuses on the imperialist heartland—not the victims of global capitalism.

Eco-Reformism: A Bourgeois Ideology

In January 2019, the American Central Intelligence Agency (CIA) issued its Worldwide Threat Assessment to guide policymakers. Alongside phony "risks" to U.S. hegemony like "international terrorism," the report frets over the very real concerns the ruling class has about the coming climate catastrophe:

"Climate hazards such as extreme weather, higher temperatures,

Steel factory in Wuhan. China is the world's largest emitter of greenhouse gases.

droughts, floods, wildfires, storms, sea level rise, soil degradation, and acidifying oceans are intensifying, threatening infrastructure, health, and water and food security. Irreversible damage to ecosystems and habitats will undermine the economic benefits they provide, worsened by air, soil, water, and marine pollution."

Among the challenges facing U.S. capitalists and their state, the report predicts that climate change will generate "competition for resources, economic distress, and social discontent," i.e., radical movements that could topple the established order. Given what is at stake, it is not surprising that political currents have emerged within bourgeois politics in the imperialist countries to address climate change.

Over the past decade, a pseudo-radical ideology has coalesced around the idea of somehow "greening" capitalism in its era of decay. Democratic Congresswoman Alexandria Ocasio-Cortez, associated with the Democratic Socialists of America (DSA), co-sponsored a "Green New Deal" resolution that died on the floor of the United States Senate in March 2019. The resolution, introduced the previous month, called for a transition to a zero-emission economy within 10 years alongside promises of full employment and universal healthcare. Although many Democratic

Bernie Sanders and Alexandria Ocasio-Cortez push pseudo-radical "Green New Deal."

politicians supported the resolution, Nancy Pelosi, the Speaker of the House of Representatives, distanced herself from the plan supposedly on the grounds that it "goes beyond" saving the planet to include reforms that might benefit ordinary working people (*Rolling Stone,* 27 February 2019). Ocasio-Cortez's claim to be a "socialist" must be set against the fact that she voted for Pelosi, whom she has since affectionately called the "mama bear of the Democratic Party."

U.S. Senator Bernie Sanders presented his own version of a Green New Deal during his campaign to win the nomination of the thoroughly capitalist Democratic Party for President of the United States. Sanders promised to lead "the decade of the Green New Deal, a ten-year, nation-wide mobilization centered around justice and equity during which climate change will be factored into virtually every area of policy, from immigration to trade to foreign policy and beyond" (berniesanders.com). Claiming to bring about "complete decarbonization of the economy by 2050 at latest," Sanders offered a raft of reforms to promote the use of renewable energy sources and make fossil fuel companies pay more in taxes and penalties.

Sanders' perspective—explicitly linked to the public-works program of Franklin Delano Roosevelt's Democratic Party of the 1930s—is intended to offer American capitalism a way to reform itself in the face of looming challenges from the left. Roosevelt sought to preclude the emergence of a revolutionary socialist movement by offering jobs to the unemployed and granting union rights to workers fighting to organize. Sanders envisions all of that plus a plan to transition to a carbon-free economy. His program aims, in fact, to channel mass discontent into the Democratic Party and the "safe" confines of rotting bourgeois democracy, even if he is not himself the candidate, injecting life into the system and defusing support for the only kind of movement that can actually defeat the "billionaire class."

For its part, the DSA enthusiastically supports Sanders' "groundbreaking" Green New Deal, both as a set of policies in its own right and as a step toward its preferred vision of "ecosocialism." The DSA observed: "Creating a fully ecological society will require a revolutionary transformation to replace the capitalist social order based on exploitation and oppression with a new society based on cooperation, equity, and justice." Indeed—but the DSA does not offer a vision of, let alone a strategy to achieve, a "revolutionary transformation" to replace capitalism with socialism. While calling to "Nationalize fossil fuel producers to phase them out as quickly as necessary" and even nodding in the direction of "workers' democratic control," the DSA promotes a reformist perspective of "worker-owned and worker-controlled cooperatives and enterprises at all levels of the economy," increased taxes and shifting priorities within the framework of the existing state:

> "Redistribute resources from the worst polluters with just and progressive taxes on the rich, on big corporations, and on dirty industry, as well as by diverting funds away from policing, prisons, and our government's bloated military budget, which have nothing to do with defense of people living within American borders and everything to do with maintaining imperial dominance over other nations and capitalist control of the world's resources. United States monetary policy has financed endless wars and wealth

extraction by elites for long enough—it's time to use it to fund the transformation we need."

—"An Ecosocialist Green New Deal: Guiding Principles,"
28 February 2019

The DSA's "revolutionary transformation" essentially boils down to electing more "progressive" Members of Congress and Bernie Sanders as President of the United States. DSA National Director Maria Svart claimed that the Vermont senator "knows what it will take to win our country back from the capitalist class" (dsausa.org). Rather than taking power out of the hands of the capitalist class (which has always controlled the country), Sanders, Ocasio-Cortez and the DSA leadership that supports them are working to ensure that no movement can emerge to overturn the system.

Eco-reformist ideology has, unsurprisingly, also found strong representation inside the social democratic British Labour Party. Under Jeremy Corbyn, Labour lost the last parliamentary election despite campaigning on a comparatively radical platform of reforms, including its own Green New Deal or "Green Industrial Revolution." While Labour's manifesto included many supportable reforms, its eco-reformist promise to bring "our energy and water systems into democratic public ownership" offered a tepid response to the crisis. Even the somewhat more radical demands approved by the membership at the party's most recent conference (Labour for a Green New Deal) fell well short of calling for the immediate expropriation of the energy companies and central economic planning by a workers' government. The political function of parties like Labour, particularly when led by left-talking reformists like Corbyn, is to ensure that the burning fire of mass discontent is snuffed out on the floor of parliament (see "Put Labour to the Test," bolshevik.org).

Unfortunately, most of the organizations that position themselves to the left of Labour and the DSA are themselves pushing a reformist perspective to address environmental and economic problems, albeit with a pseudo-revolutionary veneer. A prime example is the U.S. group Socialist Alternative (SAlt), which (together with other national sections) recently broke from the Committee for a Workers' International (CWI), with both sides of the split tenuously claiming to stand in the tradition of Lenin and Trotsky:

"We must take on the capitalist system itself. This would have to involve, as a first step, taking the energy companies, transport, agribusiness and major industry out of the hands of the profiteers. A system of workers control and management would be able to lay down the basis for an international democratic socialist plan of sustainable production, based on the need of people and planet and not of an exploiting elite."

—Socialist Alternative, 27 August 2019

Despite this declaration, SAlt's real strategy is to push existing mass movements to the left and use the mechanisms of the capitalist state to begin implementing its "socialist plan of sustainable production"—only then projecting the need for a revolutionary workers' party and a workers' state to carry through with the plan. This fake-Marxist strategy, which drags in the notion of independent working-class organizing only to cover up for a policy that contradicts it, is nowhere more evident than in SAlt's assertion that "We need to mobilize the widest possible forces to go all out for a Sanders victory" in the 2020 primaries. SAlt was unfazed by Sanders's decision to compete for the Democratic nomination despite their request that he run independently, which they correctly view as a bourgeois party. Similarly, their former comrades in the CWI supported Corbyn's efforts to become Britain's prime minister despite the CWI's (incorrect) view that Labour became a bourgeois party in the 1990s.

The political alchemists of Socialist Alternative claim that "for the Democrats to become the party we need … they would have to stop taking corporate money period, adopt a pro-working class platform and require that their representatives support it, and create real democratic structures whereby the base of the party could control its leadership." They built a political fantasy around the idea of a Sanders presidency:

"Sanders has stated that as president he will be the 'organizer in chief,' that he will mobilize working people in all areas where recalcitrant politicians refuse to do what is in the interests of their constituents. This is absolutely correct but to build this force that can keep the politicians under pressure also means having a credible threat to replace them, in other words a new party."

—Socialist Alternative, 22 December 2019

The idea that a revolutionary workers' party is going to grow out of

President Sanders's Democratic administration mobilizing for a Green New Deal is ludicrous—an unserious projection that only the politically naïve or cynical would even suggest.

The International Marxist Tendency (IMT), which split with the CWI in the 1990s, struck a more radical posture, describing the Green New Deal, as advocated in the U.S. by Sanders and Ocasio-Cortez, as "a Keynesian strategy of attempting to regulate and manage the capitalist system." They correctly note that "capitalism cannot be managed. It cannot be tamed and made 'green'...."

Yet while ostensibly rejecting the notion that the Democratic Party could be transformed into a revolutionary socialist formation, the IMT has projected that Sanders "could serve as a catalyst for a break with the Democrats that could potentially unleash forces that could get out of the control of the ruling class—and that this could open the road to a struggle for genuine socialism and revolution" (In Defence of Marxism, 18 October 2019).

Engaging with supporters of Bernie Sanders (including the DSA) and/ or with young climate change activists means finding common ground on concrete issues for struggle, and it means laying out a clear and realistic approach to building a revolutionary workers' party—not pandering to them by spinning fantasies that would convert their fundamentally flawed strategies into half-correct tactics.

In Britain, the IMT backed the Labour party in the last election. But rather than arguing that revolutionaries seek to put reformists like Corbyn in power to expose the mass illusions that he creates, the IMT portrayed a possible Labour victory as an opportunity for Marxists to give advice about how best to implement the party's manifesto and even reform capitalism out of existence:

> "If Labour is to guarantee the reforms that it has promised, then it needs to break with capitalism. This was the vision of the old Clause 4 from 1918, which talked about the need for the common ownership of the means of production, distribution and exchange....
>
> "The only way a Labour government can put an end to this nightmare is to introduce bold socialist measures to take over the economy. This means nationalisation of the banks, finance houses, land and the giant corporations that dominate our economy.

"This should be done by introducing emergency legislation. There should be no compensation to the fat cats. Industry must be planned under democratic workers' control and management. This would allow us to run the economy on the basis of need and not profit....

"We cannot wait any longer. The task of the next Labour government is to carry through the socialist transformation of society."
—In Defence of Marxism, 22 November 2019

Instead of illusory calls for "emergency legislation" introduced by a bourgeois parliament, the "socialist transformation of society," and the move to a form of development that sustains the environment as well as humanity, requires a revolutionary rupture with the capitalist state. This can only be achieved by mobilizing the mass of the population under the leadership of a revolutionary workers' party, built in opposition to the reformist Labour misleaders.

It's the Same Transition

Centered on the student strikes inspired by Swedish teenager Greta Thunberg, masses of young people have taken to the streets around the world to demand government action to avert the climate catastrophe. There is a growing awareness, particularly acute and anguished among youth, that we are rushing toward the edge of a cliff—and there is a sharpening understanding that political and economic powers are pushing us to run forward faster (while they claim to favor slowing down). When Australian Prime Minister Scott Morrison visited New South Wales, ravaged by the sort of wildfires that will only multiply with climate change, he was confronted by angry residents who extended to the Liberal Party leader such greetings as "You're an idiot" and "You're not welcome, you fuckwit!" (*Guardian*, 2 January 2020).

Revolutionaries share the frustration, worry and hatred felt by millions of ordinary working people around the world when they consider the climate crisis. But we do not promote a politics of despair. The Marxist political program offers a way forward, and that is why we intervene in climate protests to advance a perspective of socialist revolution. Sometimes we choose not to participate in actions on the grounds thatthey are misguided or even reactionary, e.g., Extinction Rebellion activists blocking a commuter train carrying ordinary people trying to get to work, advocating a strategy of mass arrests and encouraging illusions in the police. Most climate protests are, however, opportunities to raise awareness of the crisis, and we march alongside other activists who may hold very different views.

Some young activists are starting to grasp the idea that capitalism is incompatible with preserving the environment, though few have reached the understanding that centralized planning will be necessary to create a viable future. Many activists influenced by anarchism restrict themselves to denouncing capitalism while rejecting the need for a revolutionary party to overthrow it. The Green Anti-Capitalist Front, which recently made headlines in Britain by occupying a disused police station in West London, declared in a seven-point manifesto that "capitalism is the crisis," yet they call merely for "collective power," "horizontal structures" and "a new system." None of this will be enough to implement the global planning necessary in the fields of scientific research, transportation, energy generation and distribution, agriculture, manufacturing, etc. The transition to a sustainable economy is the transition to a socialist economy—a transition that can only be brought about by a working-class seizure of power.

Why the working class? At this point in the struggle against climate change, a substantial proportion of activists hitting the streets have been students (albeit many from working-class backgrounds), while Indigenous peoples (many of them also workers) have been at the forefront of protests to fight oil pipelines and fossil fuel extractions that threaten their traditional way of life. The working class as an identifiable organized force has been largely absent. Yet it is the working class that holds the solution to humanity's crisis due to the mechanisms of capitalism. As we noted in our article, "Communism & Ecology" (1917 No. 36, bolshevik.org):

> "The historical agency for communist transformation is the proletariat—'a class with radical chains.' In order to liberate itself from these chains, Marx observed, the working class has no choice but to collectivize private property and reorder the relations of production in an egalitarian and democratic manner. Insofar as there is an identity between communism and environmentally sustainable development, a political project capable of

effectively addressing ecological crises must have as its goal the seizure of power by the working class and the imposition of what Marx called *'the revolutionary dictatorship of the proletariat.'"*

Most workers today have no understanding of this historical mission. Generations of political misleadership by reformist "socialists" and trade-union bureaucrats have taken their toll. The discrepancy between the objective interests of the working class (which can only truly be met by socialism) and the subjective appreciation of the problem by individual workers is wide. Given the short timeframe the climate crisis imposes, there is ample reason to be pessimistic that the working class will be able to develop the necessary revolutionary consciousness in time to avert catastrophe.

And yet....

History shows that rapid and unexpected changes in political consciousness can occur as the result of crises (e.g., war, economic downturns). It is just possible that the climate crisis can help precipitate a sudden awareness on the part of the masses—not only that corporations and mainstream politicians have no solution—but that the problem is an economic system that necessarily privileges the enrichment of a small

Political logic of XR's reformist approach to ending climate change under capitalism.

stratum of social parasites over any other consideration. Whether due to the collapse of the global economy, an inter-imperialist war, a global pandemic (see "A Revolutionary Response to COVID-19," bolshevik.org), the onset of ecological failure or some combination of these scenarios, capitalism will at some point produce a breakdown in the normal operation of the ideological and repressive mechanisms of social contro—setting the scene for a revolutionary situation.

Such a breakdown is, however, not enough. Revolutionary opportunities have often slipped through the fingers of the working class because its existing leadership was unequal to the task of seizing power. One can cite many painful examples: Germany, 1919–1923; Spain, 1936; France, 1936 and 1968. But there is only a single example of the contrary: Russia, October 1917 (see *Celebrating Red October*, bolshevik.org). The Bolshevik party of Lenin and Trotsky was equal to the task, armed with a firm Marxist program and a leadership schooled in revolutionary tactics. The opening shot of worldwide socialist revolution rang out across the vastness of the Tsarist Empire. Its sound still echoes in the hearts of those who understand that capitalism cannot help but provoke future attempts to "storm heaven."

Working to build a revolutionary party—in meetings, on demonstrations, in workplace struggles and in campaigns against specific instances of environmental destruction, austerity or oppression, fighting against the trade-union bureaucrats and the "socialist" pretenders in the reformist parties—is the only effective contribution we can make to solving the climate change crisis. Fighting to prevent more drastic climate change and deal with the consequences we are already facing means fighting for a workers' government, not a "Green New Deal" facelift of capitalism.

Revolutionaries seek to bridge the gap between workers' current consciousness and felt needs on the one hand, and their seizure of power as a class on the other. We advance a program that follows the method of Trotsky's *Transitional Program* (see bolshevik.org/tp), raising demands to address environmental destruction as well as other maladies of capitalism, which could include:

1. massively increasing wages (doubling and tripling those at the lower end of the scale) and ensuring they keep pace or exceed the rate of inflation;

2. ending unemployment and underemployment with a significantly reduced workweek with no loss in pay at the new higher rates;
3. identifying and terminating millions of "bullshit jobs" created by the regime of private property (e.g., socially useless or even harmful roles performed by unenthusiastic people in marketing, consulting, insurance, management and other areas) and replacing them with socially-beneficial careers in the rapidly growing old and new industries of human and ecologically sustainable development;
4. implementing and massively expanding free, high-quality public education at all levels, as well as medical and other social programs;
5. assisting those people who migrate across borders for environmental, economic or personal reasons by welcoming and integrating them into the common endeavor of social improvement;
6. agitating for the defeat of imperialist powers and the defense of those who fall victim to the rulers of a global economic order based on exploitation, pillage and the destruction of the environment;
7. expropriating Big Oil, car manufacturers and aviation/military companies like Boeing to help pay for a dramatic reduction in CO_2 emissions by building extensive new networks of free public transportation to reduce the use of private vehicles and redesigning housing, workplaces and urban landscapes to reduce long commutes and other unnecessary travel;
8. cancelling all debts owed by working people, students, poor farmers and small business people to financial institutions;
9. expropriating those financial institutions and large industrial corporations, redirecting funds to a globally unified emergency research and development plan to overhaul manufacturing processes and develop alternative energy sources and technologies to reduce the effects of climate change;
10. enforcing workers' control of production at the firm level and linking industries through regionally, nationally and globally coordinated networks of workers' planning;
11. disbanding the police and military and organizing workers' emergency response units to swiftly deal with immediate physical danger caused by environmental degradation (e.g., flooding,

Firefighters battle deadly Australian wildfires that ravaged the country in 2019-20.

wildfires) or reactionary resistance to the transition (e.g., fascist squads);

12. waging a political struggle to expose the reformist misleaders and trade-union bureaucrats as we build a mass revolutionary workers' party; and

13. organizing "transition" councils in workplaces and neighborhoods as a form of workers' democracy, the basis for a workers' government to coordinate socialist transformation in the context of international cooperation.

Capitalists and their "sheepdogging" reformists will say that these things "go too far," that they are "impossible." They are only impossible for capitalism. In 1921, the revolutionary Communist International passed a resolution—drafted by the Russian delegation headed by Lenin and Trotsky—that noted the incompatibility of the needs of the working class and the needs of the capitalist system. Today, we can add that the needs of the planet are also in opposition to the needs of capitalism and let ourselves be guided by the ringing words of that resolution:

"In place of the minimum programme of the centrists and reformists, the Communist International offers a struggle for the concrete demands of the proletariat which, in their totality, challenge the power of the bourgeoisie, organize the proletariat and mark out the different stages of the struggle for its dictatorship. Even before the broad masses consciously understand the need for the dictatorship of the proletariat, they can respond to each of the individual demands. As more and more people are drawn into the struggle around these demands and as the needs of the masses come into conflict with the needs of capitalist society, the working class will come to realize that if it wants to live, capitalism will have to die."

> —cited in "Revolutionary Continuity and Transitional Demands,"
> bolshevik.org

Reprinted from *1917* No. 42 (2020)

COMMUNISM & ECOLOGY

Human emancipation & the materialist conception of history

IBT presentation to a panel discussion on capital, history and ecology.

THE STRUGGLE FOR HUMAN EMANCIPATION in the "Anthropocene," the geologic epoch distinguished by the impact of civilization on the natural environment, is inextricably bound up with the project of establishing an egalitarian and ecologically sustainable economic order. In seeking to understand the evolution of human society and the possibility of realizing this new order, i.e., communism, Marx developed the materialist conception of history.

Marx did not engage in a moralistic denunciation of exploitation and human bondage in the abstract. Oppression is as old as class-divided society itself, and its historical origins have been addressed by theologians and idealist philosophers—but until Marx, no one was able to explain the material and social foundations of the appearance, persistence and eventual disappearance of class divisions.

Key to the materialist conception of history, and the practical project of transcending class society, is the concept of the *forces of production*. In *The German Ideology*, Marx and Engels observed that humanity, at a certain stage in its evolution, began to *produce* its means of subsistence. Other animals do this to a limited extent, but production has fundamentally shaped our species.

Production is essentially the transformation of natural objects by human activity into useful things, aka use-values, or "wealth." As such, it can be considered a process of "material exchange" or conversion occurring *within* nature. Momentum is generated in the first instance through the dialectical antagonism between the two sides of the exchange, i.e., humanity and the rest of nature. In his useful (albeit flawed) book, *Marx's Ecology*, John Bellamy Foster correctly stresses the centrality of this concept of material exchange—or human-nature "metabolism"—to Marx's materialism, and cites his important observation in *Capital* that "Labour is, first of all, a process between man and nature, a process by which man, through his own actions, mediates, regulates and controls the metabolism between himself and nature."

The "metabolic" conversion of matter by human labor requires means of production. Combined with technique, labor power and forms of organization, these means of production are the basis of Marx's concept of the productive forces, i.e., human capacities to transform nature. The speed, efficiency, form and purpose of the metabolic conversion, as well as its ultimate sustainability, are dependent on the complex interplay of the forces and social relations of production that together constitute historically distinct modes of production.

The history of the progress of human civilization, Marx argued in 1859, can be traced in the development of the forces of production through successive modes of production. "Primitive communism," humanity's initial mode of production, was essentially egalitarian in structure and its distribution of social wealth. But this was an "equality of poverty," because the "primitive" productive forces yielded little more than basic subsistence, and humans therefore remained hostage to the vagaries of nature.

While the causes of the transition to class society remain obscure, it is clear that the material foundation of class division—with the attendant gender inequality and other forms of servitude—was the development of productive forces to the point that it was possible for a tiny privileged section of the population to exist without directly participating in production.

Henceforth the drive to enhance labor productivity—or to increase the efficiency of the human-nature metabolism—was mediated by non-egalitarian social relations. Beyond the need to "master" the forces of nature in order to protect the community from predators and other dan-

Child sifts through discarded electronic components in a toxic waste dump near Accra, Ghana.

gers, a social imperative to develop the productive forces had also been introduced insofar as the ruling stratum sought to increase its wealth at the expense of the laboring majority, the "direct producers." While this social imperative was deforming (and frequently counterproductive), the historically changing class-based logics of surplus appropriation nonetheless led to the progressive, if non-linear, augmentation of human capacities through what Marx described as the "Asiatic, ancient, feudal, and modern bourgeois modes of production."

Capitalism, more than any previous class-divided mode of production, has enormously accelerated the development of the material forces of production, but it has done so not to expand the quantities of use-values, but in order to maximize profit—with complete disregard for "wealth," including the natural environment. Foster, following Marx, argues that the logic of capitalism (which is essentially anarchic and led by "blind" economic forces operating "behind the backs" of human beings) is detached from the material-human world on which it ultimately rests—leading to metabolic or ecological "rifts" through the same social process that Marx described as the self-alienation of labor.

Capitalism has taken alienation, exploitation and inequality to unprecedented heights while providing humanity for the first time with the possibility of eliminating these scourges through a fundamental reorganization of the social relations of production. In Marx's words, capitalism has "create[d] the material conditions for the solution" of social antagonisms. While widening ecological rifts to an extremely dangerous extent, and thereby imperiling the very foundations of human existence, capitalism has also "created the material conditions" to repair those rifts, if the bourgeois mode of production can be eliminated before it destroys the environmental preconditions for human life on Earth.

Ecology, 'Growth' & the Transition to Communism

Marxism provides a guide for the historical transformation of society through struggling for changes that both initiate the transition to communism and anticipate its early stages. In the *Critique of the Gotha Program*, Marx brilliantly sketches a transitional period between capitalism and the lower phase of communism, which Lenin and others characterized as "socialism," during which society will still be "economically, morally and intellectually... stamped with the birth-marks of the old society from whose womb it emerges." Nevertheless, the collective ownership of the means of production will represent a fundamental transformation in the economic foundations of society, vastly enhancing humanity's capacity to control nature.

Capitalism is enormously wasteful, all the more so in the epoch of its decline, with an increasing proportion of human activity devoted to financial speculation, marketing, military expenditures and other irrational overheads that the "free market" requires. The reorganization of economic activity on the basis of a rational plan would immediately increase efficiency, reduce waste and dramatically improve the lives, and tap the energy and ability, of the billions of human beings whom capitalism has consigned to hopeless poverty and privation.

Marx projected that the continuing development of the socialist mode of production would ultimately result in full communism—i.e., a classless, stateless order—in which society will "inscribe on its banners: From each according to his ability, to each according to his needs!" Yet as Marx explains in the *Critique of the Gotha Program*, this will only happen "after the productive forces have also increased with the all-round development of the individual, and all the springs of common wealth flow more abundantly." The further *growth* of the productive forces is required to establish the material basis for the transition to communism. In *The German Ideology*, Marx and Engels explain that to transcend the alienation of class society, the "development of productive forces...is an absolutely necessary practical premise because without it *want* is merely made general, and with *destitution* the struggle for necessities and all the old filthy business would necessarily be reproduced."

Many self-styled Marxists (including Foster) advocate a "steady-state economy," and some even echo petty-bourgeois environmentalist calls for "de-growth." These perspectives are premised on the notion that the ecological destruction wrought by capitalism is a product of growth *per se*, rather than the consequence of the pursuit of profit maximization and the anarchic character of production under capitalism. Like Foster, many socialist groups tailor their treatment of sustainable development to the anti-technological and anti-growth prejudices of the green activists they seek to recruit.

Capitalism has of course developed the productive forces without regard for ensuring the well-being of our species and its ability to co-exist with the natural environment. But even some of the more dangerous technologies and practices (such as nuclear fission) might be adapted to contribute to humane, sustainable development in a rationally planned economy in which the "associated producers" factor in the environmental effects of particular technologies in their decision-making.

Anti-growth advocates generally reject the expansion of productive capacity on essentially moral grounds. Some environmentalists even favor a return to more primitive economic models and propose that the population of the advanced capitalist countries lower their standard of

Poverty and privation outside a slum in Mumbai, India.

living while those in the "developing" world should curb their expectations. Such notions are both reactionary and utopian, and have nothing in common with Marxism, which holds that only through the further development of the productive forces will it be possible to eliminate class contradictions and the unregulated, destructive interaction of humanity and nature.

In his *Economic and Philosophic Manuscripts of 1844*, Marx described communism as "the *genuine* resolution of the conflict between man and nature and between man and man—the true resolution of the strife between existence and essence, between objectification and self-confirmation, between freedom and necessity, between the individual and the species. Communism is the riddle of history solved, and it knows itself to be this solution."

Proletarian Centrality & Revolutionary Organization

The historical agency for communist transformation is the proletariat—"a class with *radical chains*." In order to liberate itself from these chains, Marx observed, the working class has no choice but to collectivize private property and reorder the relations of production in an egalitarian and democratic manner. Insofar as there is an identity between communism and environmentally sustainable development, a political project capable of effectively addressing ecological crises must have as its goal the seizure of power by the working class and the imposition of what Marx called *"the revolutionary dictatorship of the proletariat."*

Yet many present-day admirers of Marx, and virtually all green activists, view this perspective as hopelessly naïve, if not outdated or even dangerous. While more pro-working class environmentalists sometimes put forward hazy calls for labor to take up the cause of sustainable growth, others are indifferent or even hostile toward working people, whom they disdain as myopic conspicuous consumers interested in maintaining the polluting factories, mines, refineries, etc., in which they work. What is necessary is an approach that links strategies to redress environmental crises and the growth of social inequality on the one hand to a perspective of the socialist reorganization of society on the other.

This requires organization—a revolutionary party capable of leading the working class and other oppressed layers to fight for state power. Building such a party must center on winning mass support for a revolutionary *program*, i.e., a set of demands that constitute a basis of practical struggle to guide the spontaneous movements of the workers and oppressed in the direction of overturning the dictatorship of the bourgeoisie and creating a new type of state based on democratic working-class institutions.

It has to be acknowledged that, with very few exceptions, even the best exponents of the Marxist tradition have paid relatively scant attention to environmental problems. In recent years the scope of ecological catastrophe has become obvious with an unambiguous consensus within the scientific community on the implications of anthropogenic climate change. Yet some self-described Marxists continue to downplay the dangers out of a misguided desire not to adapt politically to petty-bourgeois environmentalism.

Unlike mainstream climate activists, Marxists reject the idea that capitalism can be incrementally transformed into an eco-friendly system. This is not to say that revolutionaries should be indifferent to particular instances of ecological degradation—it is necessary to be actively involved in struggles to resist corporate destruction of the environment. Yet the chief responsibility of Marxists is to attempt to popularize the understanding that such destruction is a manifestation of the profound irrationality of the capitalist mode of production.

The necessity of the revolutionary transformation of society through working-class revolution has never been more urgent. Marxism offers the only realistic chance our species has for survival, because, in the end, the problems of human freedom and sustainable economic development are inseparably intertwined: both require the expropriation of the expropriators and the creation of a rationally-planned socialist economy on a world scale.

Text of a presentation to a panel discussion on capital, history and ecology held by the Platypus group at York University, Toronto.

Reprinted from *1917* No.36 (2014)

CAPITALISM VS. SCIENCE AT FOULDEN MAAR

DAILY NEWS STORIES CHRONICLE the breakdown of Earth's environment due to destructive human intervention caused by international capitalism's relentless pursuit of super-profits. Our comrades in Otago, New Zealand, have recently been involved in fighting one small manifestation of capitalism's rampage across the planet.

Opposition to mining Foulden Maar near Middlemarch began when residents of the rural community became alarmed at their quiet neighbourhood turning into a 24/7 transit route for heavy, double-articulated trucks for an estimated 27 years. It was all part of a grand money-spinning scheme by Australian/Malaysian transnational corporation Plaman Resources, which intended to use the diatomite (fossilised algae) contained in the maar (volcano crater) as a fertiliser additive for Southeast Asian palm oil plantations, and as a stock feed additive for factory farms

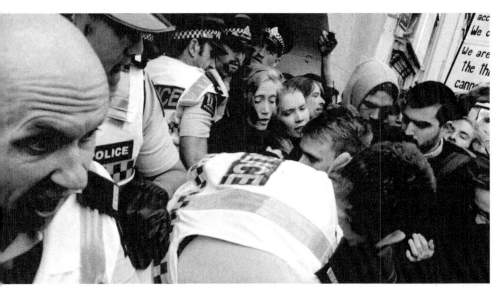

*Police clash with protesters during Minerals Forum outside Dunedin Town Hall in Otago, New Zealand, May 2019. **Previous page:** Plaman Resources planned to mine the white diatomite at Foulden Maar, destroying invaluable climate change data and fossils.*

and feedlots. But as the scientific and geological importance of the site became publicly known, opposition has grown dramatically over the last six months to include leftists, community activists and climate-change fighters.

Foulden Maar is a 23-million-year-old volcanic crater that over time filled seasonally with layers of diatoms—the fossilised remains of single-celled algae composed of silica. The tiny part of the maar which has so far been explored by scientists already reveals a huge range of fossils of plants, fish, insects and spiders caught between the layers of algae. They are so well preserved due to the anoxic environment of the 180-metre-deep crater that, in some cases, tissue and DNA still remains in the fossils. From these, it is possible to extrapolate the prehistoric biosphere in this part of the world.

Of global importance given the impact of climate change, Foulden Maar also holds within its layers of sediment an extraordinary record of climatic fluctuations on a season-by-season basis. As the only known record of such detail from a time when the Antarctic last went through a period of rapid deglaciation, this is of global practical importance in interpreting current climatic trends. International paleoclimatologist Beth Fox describes the site as:

> "the only record that can document this period on human timescales, i.e. over periods of seasons to centuries. The more information we have about how the Earth system has responded to past changes in carbon dioxide and Antarctic ice volume, the better."
>
> — Letter to Save Foulden Maar campaign group, 5 August 2019

All this was at risk of being completely destroyed in a saga of greed and deceit by a cast of nefarious characters—from politicians willing to sacrifice Foulden Maar for short term economic gain and limited employment opportunities, to the ultra-rich whose way of life is dependent on exploiting both the world's limited resources and the labour and lives of the working class.

Local businesses, politicians and bureaucrats swooned at the prospect of a share of the hundreds of millions of dollars investment promised by the Plaman directors, two smooth-talking Australian bankers-cum-entrepreneurs related to some of the biggest property developers in Sydney, with backing from Malaysian tech giant Iris Corporation and seed funding from multinational investment bank Goldman Sachs. Official Information Act requests showed Plaman wheeling and dealing with bureaucrats in Kiwi Rail, the Ministry of Business, Innovation and Employment, the Ministry of Trade and Enterprise and Clutha District Council in a strategy to access the publicly financed Provincial Growth Fund to build infrastructure without which, it later transpired, they could not economically mine Foulden Maar.

A leaked document showed that former Labour Party politician Clayton Cosgrove had been engaged by Plaman as a "government relations advisor" for his "outstanding relationships with the ruling Labour Government" to curry favour and ease Plaman Resources through compliance (*Otago Daily Times*, 20 April 2019). None of these politicians or bureaucrats did their due diligence in relation to the company and its claims, or investigated the site itself. But both the politicians and the corporation underestimated the opposition. Plaman had gone to great

Geologists at Foulden Maar clean fossils which are held between layers of diatomite.

lengths to avoid alerting the public of the geological importance of Foulden Maar and had not anticipated their duplicity being revealed. The political furore drove Plaman Resources into liquidation in July. While this buys time, the land is still in private hands. A scientific reserve under public ownership is necessary to preserve the maar.

Foulden Maar has become yet another symbol of the rapaciousness and irrationality of capitalism in its pursuit of short-term profit at the cost of long-term survival. There are sites of scientific and historic interest all over the world similarly at risk, and the workers' movement must actively intervene to defend them. Foulden Maar is of particular interest because the data it contains will help scientists studying the effects of climate change. After a hard fight, it may be possible to retain and study this important data even under capitalism. But taking effective action to prevent what climate scientists are forecasting is not possible while the world is run for profit (see "Communism & Ecology", bolshevik.org).

Capitalism cannot be fixed. We must build a revolutionary international to overthrow capitalism worldwide. Our only hope is a global economic plan under workers' rule to manage resources in the interests of the planet and all its occupants. Small victories like saving Foulden Maar can be used as a bridge toward those ends.

Reprinted from *1917* No.42 (2020)

Update November 2020

PLAMAN RESOURCES, THE TRANSNATIONAL that planned a destructive mining operation at the site, has now been in receivership for 14 months, and efforts to bring the maar into public ownership have been protracted as "good faith" negotiations between receivers and the Dunedin City Council have gone beyond the legal 12 month time limit.

The scientific importance of Foulden Maar in understanding climate change continues to grow with the publication of a recent paper in the prestigious European Geosciences Union journal *Climate of the Past* ("Elevated CO_2, increased leaf-level productivity, and water-use efficiency during the early Miocene," Tammo Reichgelt et al, August 2020). But for the first time in five decades scientists have been refused access to the site with no reason given by the receivers.

Researchers have only just scratched the surface of the information that could be revealed at the site. Only under public ownership, which would allow scientists not to work around the goodwill (so easily withdrawn) and commercial imperatives of a privately-owned company, would the true extent of Foulden Maar's fossil treasures and climate change data be fully realized.

International Bolshevik Tendency

WHO WE ARE

WE STAND FOR WORKING-CLASS REVOLUTION to overthrow capitalism on a global scale. Our vision is a world without hunger, war and oppression, in which all human beings may develop their full potential while protecting the environment on which we depend.

We take our inspiration from the 1917 Russian Revolution, the only time the working class has succeeded in taking power. Red October demonstrated the need for a disciplined party of revolutionaries committed to a clear Marxist program and for independent political action by the working class, as opposed to coalitions with bourgeois parties (popular fronts).

Despite Stalinist degeneration, we defended the Soviet Union against internal and external capitalist threats until its destruction in August 1991, while advocating political revolution to replace the bureaucracy with workers' power. The same applies to the "deformed workers' states" of China, Cuba, Vietnam and North Korea today.

Trotsky's principled fight against Stalinism led in 1938 to the founding of the Fourth International, which was soon destroyed by a political current (Pabloism) that sought to replace the struggle for a mass vanguard party with pressuring Stalinists, social democrats and bourgeois nationalists to the left—an orientation promoted by most groups claiming to be Trotskyist today.

We fight oppression in all its forms, whether based on race, nationality, gender, sexuality, age, health or ability. We reject ideologies that advocate political unity across classes such as nationalism and feminism, though we may work with people from these traditions in actions that benefit the oppressed. We defend the right of nations to self-determination and side militarily with neocolonial forces attacked by imperialism.

In strikes, demonstrations and united-front actions, we are on the side of the oppressed, advancing a program for workers' power. The greatest obstacle to socialist revolution is the misleadership of the working class: reformists, anarchists and centrists who wittingly or unwittingly defend the existing order.

The IBT is a small organization with big ambitions. We seek to advance a program that will not only recruit individuals but act as a catalyst for realignments within existing organizations, create new ones through principled fusion and ultimately reforge the Fourth International, world party of socialist revolution.

Printed in Great Britain
by Amazon

21867549R10031